AN ARK FULL OF RECIPES

For my mother, with love

AN ARK FULL OF RECIPES

CLAIRE FREEDMAN

Marshall Pickering
An Imprint of HarperCollinsPublishers

ACKNOWLEDGEMENTS

My grateful thanks go to Rabbi Mendel Lew of the Southend and Westcliff Hebrew Congregation, for taking time out of his busy schedule to help me with the section on the Jewish Passover and Seder.

Marshall Pickering is an Imprint of HarperCollins*Religious*

Part of HarperCollins*Publishers*

77–85 Fulham Palace Road, London W6 8JB

First published in Great Britain in 1999 by Marshall Pickering

1 3 5 7 9 10 8 6 4 2

Copyright © 1999 Claire Freedman

Claire Freedman asserts the moral right to be identified as the author of this work.

A catalogue record for this book is available from the British Library.

ISBN 0 551 03200 6

Printed and bound in Great Britain by Woolnough Bookbinding Ltd, Irthlingborough, Northamptonshire

CONDITIONS OF SALE
This book is sold subject to the condition that it shall not, by way of trade or otherwise, be lent, re-sold, hired out or otherwise circulated without the publisher's prior consent in any form of binding or cover other than that in which it is published and without a similar condition including this condition being imposed on the subsequent purchaser.

All rights reserved. No part of this publication may be reproduced, stored in a retrieval system, or transmitted, in any form or by any means, electronic, mechanical, photocopying, recording or otherwise, without the prior permission of the publishers.

CONTENTS

COOK'S RULES — 7

1. THE CREATION — 8
Sun, Moon and Stars Cookies — 9

2. ADAM AND EVE — 11
Adam's Tempting Toffee Apples — 12
Spotty Serpents — 13

3. NOAH AND THE ARK — 15
Noah's Arks — 16

4. ESAU AND JACOB — 18
Jacob's Potage — 19

5. MOSES IN THE BULRUSHES — 20
Babies in Baskets — 21

6. MOSES IS CALLED BY GOD — 22
Pharaoh's Pyramids — 23

7. THE PLAGUES OF EGYPT — 24
Frogs in Rivers of Blood — 25

8. THE LAST PLAGUE — 26
The Jewish Passover — 26
Charoset — 28
Cinnamon Balls — 28
Matzo Fritters — 29

9. FOOD IN THE DESERT — 30
'Manna' Ices — 31

10. A LAND FLOWING WITH MILK AND HONEY — 32
Milk and Honey Ice-cream — 33
Milk and Honey Dreamy Desert Drink — 34
Milk and Honey Fluff — 34

11. THE FRUITS OF THE PROMISED LAND — 35
Figgy Flapjacks — 36
Bible Fruits Compote — 37

12. AARON'S STAFF — 38
Aaron's Almond Shortbread — 39
Almond and Raisin Fudge — 40

13. BARAK'S VICTORIOUS BATTLE — 41
Sisera's 'Stuck in the Mud' Pudding — 42
Sisera's Chariot-Wheel Quiche — 43
Mudslide Shakes — 44

14. THE STORY OF RUTH — 45
Ruth's Straw Bundles — 46

15. KING SOLOMON — 47
Solomon's Golden Shields — 48
Solomon's Bowls of Gold — 49
King's Royal Crowns — 50

16. THE QUEEN OF SHEBA — 51
The Queen of Sheba's '3 Spices' Honey Cake — 52
Cinnamon Toast — 53
Ginger Spiced Apples — 53

17. ELIJAH AND THE BARREL OF CORN — 54
Elijah's Barrels of Corn — 55

18. THE STORY OF ESTHER — 56
Hamantaschen ('Haman's Purses') — 57

19. DANIEL IN THE LIONS' DEN — 58
Daniel's Roaring Lion Tarts — 59

20. JONAH AND THE GREAT FISH — 61
Jonah's Fun Fish Cakes — 62
Jonah's Fish and Ships — 63
Deep Sea Jellies — 64

COOK'S RULES

Before you start cooking, always remember these important rules.

1. Do not cook anything unless there is an adult in the kitchen to help you.
2. Read each recipe before you start, to make sure you have everything you need.
3. Wash your hands and put on an apron.
4. Weigh and measure all the ingredients carefully.
5. Always wear oven gloves when putting things into or taking them out of the oven, or when picking up anything hot.
6. Always turn saucepan handles to the side of the cooker, so that you do not knock them.
7. Have a space ready to put hot pans. Put them onto a wooden board or trivet.
8. Take extra care when using sharp knives or graters.
9. Be very careful when boiling or frying anything.
10. Never leave the kitchen while the electric or gas rings are switched on.
11. Mop up any spills straight away, before someone slips on them. It also helps to clean up as you go along.
12. Always turn the oven off when you have finished cooking.

1. THE CREATION

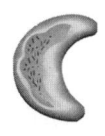

In the beginning God made the heavens and the earth. At first the earth was covered in water and was completely dark.

Then God said, 'Let there be light!' and there was light. He divided the light from the darkness and made day and night.

On earth, he turned the waters into seas to let dry land appear. He filled the land with lots of plants and trees.

'Now let lights shine in heaven, to mark days and years,' said God, and so the sun, moon and stars were created.

He filled the seas with fish and the air with birds. He also made all kinds of animals, both large and small, to live on earth.

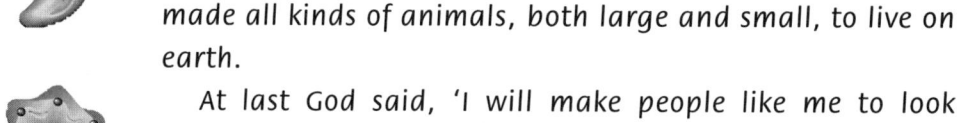

At last God said, 'I will make people like me to look after my world.' So he created men and women and blessed them.

God looked around and was pleased with his work. It had taken six days to make the world, and on the seventh day he rested.

Genesis 1–2

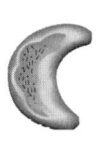

Sun, Moon and Stars Cookies

Ingredients (makes about 45)

For the biscuits

100g/4oz	**butter/soft margarine**
100g/4oz	**soft brown sugar**
1	**egg**
225g/8oz	**plain flour**
1 pinch of	**salt**
1 teaspoon	**mixed spice**

For icing and decorating

150g/5oz	**icing sugar**
1–2 tablespoons	**hot water**
	yellow food colouring
	edible silver balls
	hundreds and thousands
	small orange and yellow jelly diamonds

You will need 2 round cookie cutters (1 large, 1 small), a star-shaped cookie cutter, and a large, non-stick baking sheet.

1. Preheat the oven to gas mark 5, 190°C (375°F).
2. Grease and flour a large, non-stick baking sheet.
3. In a large mixing bowl, mix the butter and sugar together with a wooden spoon until smooth and creamy.
4. Crack open the egg into a cup, and beat. Add to the mixture of butter and sugar, stirring in well.
5. Now sift in the flour, salt and mixed spice. Mix everything together to form a dough.
6. Sprinkle some flour onto the work surface, and roll out the dough to a thickness of about 5mm/¼in. Be careful not to roll it too thinly! Use the cookie cutters to press out sun, moon and star shapes from the dough. To make the moons, cut out small circles with the larger round cutter, then, using the smaller-sized round cutter, cut part of the biscuit away to make a crescent moon shape.
7. Place the cookies on the baking sheet and put near the top of the oven. Cook for about 15 minutes or until lightly golden.
8. When the biscuits are ready, remove from the oven wearing oven gloves. Leave to cool on a wire rack.

9. Meanwhile, put the icing sugar into another bowl, adding the water a little at a time until you have an icing that will spread. Put $1/3$ of the icing into a separate bowl, add a few drops of yellow food colouring and blend well. Leave the rest of the icing white.
10. When the biscuits are completely cool, spread the yellow icing over the sun-shaped cookies using a palate knife, and do the same with the white icing for the star- and moon-shaped cookies.
11. While the icing is still wet, decorate the cookies as follows:
    Stars: Press a silver ball into the point of each star.
    Moons: Sprinkle with the hundreds and thousands.
    Suns: Place alternating yellow and orange jelly diamonds all around the edges of the cookies to make them look like 'shining suns'.
12. Leave to set before storing in an airtight tin.

2. ADAM AND EVE

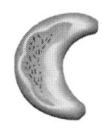

The first man and woman that God made were called Adam and Eve. They lived in a beautiful garden, called Eden, which God himself planted.

Two special trees grew in the garden: the Tree of Life and the Tree of the Knowledge of Good and Evil.

'You may eat the fruit of any tree,' God told Adam, 'but don't touch the fruit of the Tree of the Knowledge of Good and Evil or else you will die!'

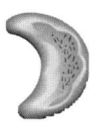

The crafty serpent knew all about this forbidden fruit. He persuaded Eve to eat some, and she gave the fruit to Adam too.

At once Adam and Eve realized that they were naked, and they tried to hide from God. But God found out and was angry.

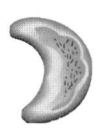

'Because you have disobeyed me,' God said, 'you will both have to work hard to get a living from the land.'

God punished the serpent, and although he still loved Adam and Eve, he would not let them enter his garden again.

Genesis 2–3

Adam's Tempting Toffee Apples

Ingredients (makes 8)

8	**apples**
225g/8oz	**granulated sugar**
225g/8oz	**golden syrup**

You will need 8 wooden sticks.

Younger children will need supervision for this recipe.

1. Wash the apples and insert the wooden sticks firmly.
2. Now grease a large, shallow dish with butter.
3. Put the sugar and golden syrup into a large, heavy-based saucepan.
4. Heat the sugar and golden syrup mixture, stirring continuously with a wooden spoon until all the sugar dissolves. Now turn up the heat and allow the mixture to boil.
5. Continue heating for about 4–5 minutes, stirring the mixture all the time until it turns a chestnut-brown colour. You can tell if the toffee is ready by testing a few drops of the mixture in a saucer of cold water. If it is still soft then it's not quite done, as you should be able to crack it between your fingers. (A sugar thermometer will register 310°F.) Remember, hot toffee can burn, so take care not to splash it on your hands!
6. When the toffee is ready, turn down the heat to the lowest setting.
7. Holding them by the wooden stick, dip the apples into the hot toffee, turning them to make sure they're covered well. Dip again for thicker toffee.
8. Place on the buttered dish and leave to set.

Spotty Serpents

Ingredients (makes 9)

75g/3oz	**soft margarine**
1	**egg**
1 teaspoon	**Marmite**
100g/4oz	**plain flour**
	a small quantity of egg white/milk for brushing
18	**small currants for the serpents' eyes**
	a small packet of poppy seeds

You will need a baking tray.

1. Grease and flour a large non-stick baking tray.
2. In a bowl, beat the margarine until soft and creamy and then stir in the beaten egg.
3. Add the Marmite (at this stage the ingredients will not blend easily).
4. Fold in the flour a little at a time to form a soft, workable dough.
5. Pull off a small lump of dough (about the size of a ping-pong ball) and roll it between your hands and on a floured board to form a sausage 15–18cm/6–7in long.
6. Round off and flatten one end to make the serpent's head. Twist the dough into an 'S' to form the body and pinch the end to make a tail. Place on the baking tray.
7. For coiled serpents: stretch the same amount of dough to a 28cm/11in long, thin sausage. Pinch one end to make the tail, coil up from the bottom and make the head as above. Place on the baking tray.
8. Chill in the fridge for 1 hour to prevent the serpents losing their shape whilst cooking.
9. Pre-heat the oven to gas mark 5, 190°C (375°F).
10. Brush the serpents with a little egg white or milk.
11. Press on the currant 'eyes' and sprinkle lightly with poppy seeds.

12. Bake in the middle of the oven for about 20–25 minutes until golden.
13. Remove from the tray while still warm and cool on a rack.
14. Store in an airtight tin. These are delicious eaten straight from the oven, or warmed up again later.

3. NOAH AND THE ARK

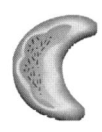

When God saw how wicked people had become, he was sorry he'd created them. He decided to destroy the world with a flood.

But one man, Noah, was good.

God told Noah, 'Build an ark, so you and your family can be spared. Take with you a pair of every kind of animal, and supplies of food.'

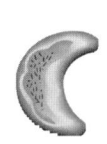

Noah obeyed God. As the last animal boarded the ark, the first drops of rain began to fall. It rained for 40 days and 40 nights and every living thing outside the ark drowned.

At last the rain stopped, and the ark ran aground on Mount Ararat. Noah sent out a raven, hoping it might find dry land and settle, but the raven returned.

So he sent out a dove, which brought back an olive leaf. He released the dove again, and when it didn't return Noah knew it was time to leave the ark.

God promised never to destroy the world by a flood again, and sent his rainbow as sign of his promise.

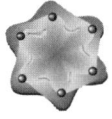

Genesis 6–9

Noah's Arks

Ingredients (makes 4)

100g/4oz	**strong cheese**
2	**large baking potatoes**
4	**chipolata sausages**
knob of	**fat for sausages**
pinch of	**salt and pepper**
420g/15oz	**can baked beans**
4 pieces of	**ham cut into 9cm/3½in squares**
knob of	**butter**
8	**cocktail sticks**

You will need 2 baking trays.

1. Pre-heat the oven to gas mark 7, 220°C (425°F).
2. Scrub the potatoes. Prick all over with a fork and place on one of the baking trays. Cook at the top of the oven for about 1 hour or until soft when squeezed (make sure you wear oven gloves when checking).
3. Meanwhile, place the sausages on the other baking tray with a little fat and cook for about half an hour with the potatoes.
4. Grate the cheese and prepare the ham slices.
5. When the potatoes are cooked, cut them in half wearing oven gloves. Scoop the filling out into a large bowl. Mash well with a fork or potato masher. Stir in the cheese, butter and the seasoning. For creamier potatoes you can add a little milk. Don't forget your sausages!
6. Place the empty potato skins back on the baking tray. Open the can of beans and put a spoonful into each skin.
7. Carefully spoon the mashed potato mixture back on top of the beans. Mould the potato to make the raised 'ark' shape. Return to the oven for about 15 minutes to warm the beans.

8. Remove the cooked sausages from the oven. To form the giraffes, cut a 4–5cm/1¾in slice from one end of each sausage. Place the small sausage piece on top of the long sausage piece. Secure with 2 cocktail sticks, leaving a bit of each cocktail stick showing at the top for the giraffe's horns.
9. Remove the potatoes from the oven. Cover the raised potato area with a slice of ham. Push the sausage giraffe in at the side. Serve at once.

4. ESAU AND JACOB

Esau and Jacob were twins – but they couldn't have been more different from each other.

Esau, the elder, became a skilful hunter. His days were spent outdoors, roaming the plains in search of deer and game.

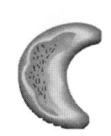

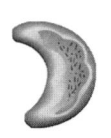

Jacob was much quieter. He preferred to stay at home. One day, while Jacob was in his tent cooking, Esau rushed in. 'Let me have some of that red lentil soup you've made,' he demanded. 'I'm starving!'

'No!' Jacob replied. 'Not unless you give me your right as the first born son, the right to inherit our father's wealth!'

Esau didn't hesitate. 'I'm about to die with hunger and exhaustion,' he cried. 'Of what use is that birthright to me now?'

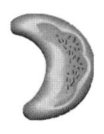

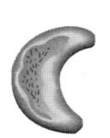

So, there and then, Esau gave his birthright over to Jacob. In exchange, Jacob gladly gave him a bowl of the soup with some bread.

Genesis 25

Jacob's Potage

Ingredients (a thick lentil soup that serves 4)

1	**onion**
2	**small carrots**
1	**leek, trimmed**
25g/1oz	**margarine**
175g/6oz	**split red lentils (non-soak variety)**
1.2 litres/ 2 pints	**water**
1	**chicken stock cube**
1 tablespoon	**tomato purée**
1 teaspoon	**mixed dried herbs**
	salt and pepper

1. Chop the carrots, onion and leek finely.
2. Heat the margarine in a large saucepan, add the vegetables and fry for about 10 minutes until the onions and leeks are soft.
3. Add the lentils, water and chicken stock cube. Gradually bring to the boil, stirring until the stock cube has dissolved.
4. Add the tomato purée, herbs and salt and pepper to taste. Turn the heat down, and simmer very gently for 30–40 minutes or until the lentils are tender but still have 'bite'. If the soup becomes too thick, more water may be added without spoiling the flavour.
5. Serve with hot crusty rolls and cheese.

5. MOSES IN THE BULRUSHES

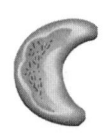

While the Israelites were slaves in Egypt, their tribes increased in size.

Pharaoh, the king of Egypt, was worried that they might become too powerful and impossible to control. So he ordered that all Israelite baby boys should be drowned in the River Nile.

But one Israelite mother hid her baby son until he grew too big to hide any longer. Then she wove a reed basket and hid him in it, amongst the bulrushes in the river.

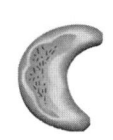

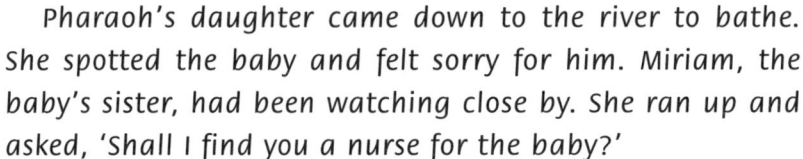

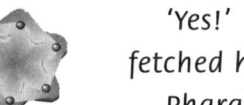

Pharaoh's daughter came down to the river to bathe. She spotted the baby and felt sorry for him. Miriam, the baby's sister, had been watching close by. She ran up and asked, 'Shall I find you a nurse for the baby?'

'Yes!' Pharaoh's daughter agreed, so Miriam ran and fetched her own mother.

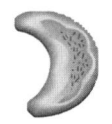

Pharaoh's daughter named the baby Moses – which means 'drawn out of the water'. Moses lived at the royal palace, but his mother never let him forget he was a Hebrew.

Exodus 1–2

Babies in Baskets

Ingredients (makes about 8)

25g/1oz	**soft margarine**
1 level tablespoon	**golden syrup**
25g/1oz	**sugar**
40g/1½oz	**cocoa powder**
8 tablespoons	**Rice Krispies**
	jelly babies

You will need a jam tart baking tin.

1. Grease the jam tart baking tin.
2. In a large saucepan, melt the margarine and golden syrup together. Do not allow to boil.
3. Add the sugar and cocoa powder. Stir well and remove from the heat.
4. Stir in the Rice Krispies, one tablespoon at a time. Make sure they are well covered with the chocolate mixture.
5. Fill the jam tart holes to the top with the mixture. Press the middle of the mixture with a teaspoon to make a basket shape.
6. Place a jelly baby in the space created. Put the jam tart baking tin in the fridge to set for an hour, and then carefully lift the baskets out.

6. MOSES IS CALLED BY GOD

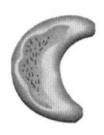

Moses grew up in luxury at Pharaoh's palace, but he soon realized that his own people weren't so fortunate. They were forced to work as slaves for the Egyptians, who treated them cruelly.

Moses left Egypt and fled to Sinai, where God spoke to him out of a burning bush.

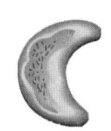

'I have seen the suffering of my people and have come to rescue them,' God said. 'I have chosen you, Moses, to lead the Israelites out of Egypt – to freedom!'

God sent Moses back to Egypt to beg Pharaoh to let his people go, but Pharaoh refused.

'How dare you think of taking away my slaves!' Pharaoh cried. 'I need them to build bricks for my pyramids and palaces!' In his anger, Pharaoh ordered the Israelites to work even harder. He stopped supplying them with the straw they needed to make bricks.

In their despair and exhaustion, the Israelites cried to Moses – and Moses spoke to God.

'Oh Lord, see what has happened now. There is no hope!'

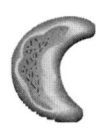

Exodus 2–5

Pharaoh's Pyramids

Ingredients (makes about 16)

2	**eggs**
225g/8oz	**desiccated coconut**
140g/5oz	**caster sugar**

You will need two large baking trays

1. Pre-heat oven to gas mark 4, 180°C (350°F).
2. Grease and flour two large baking trays (or cover the trays with greased and floured grease-proof paper).
3. Crack the eggs open into a large bowl, and lightly beat them.
4. Now add and mix in the coconut and sugar until the mixture becomes quite firm. If it is at all soggy, add a little more coconut.
5. Wet your hands in cold water, and then form the mixture into small pyramid shapes. Place the pyramids on the baking trays.
6. Bake for 15–20 minutes until the pyramids are lightly browned.
7. Leave to cool slightly before removing them from the trays.

7. THE PLAGUES OF EGYPT

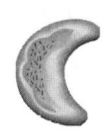

Once more, God told Moses to plead with Pharaoh for the Israelites' release. But again Pharaoh wouldn't listen.

So God said to Moses, 'Tell your brother, Aaron, to hold his staff over the River Nile.'

As Aaron did this, the waters instantly turned to blood. Seven days passed, and the fish died, making the river stink – but Pharaoh would not give in.

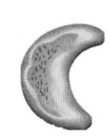

So God covered the land with frogs. They hopped and crawled inside Pharaoh's own palaces, but still he refused to give in.

Next, God made a plague of gnats out of the dust, followed by great swarms of flies to torment the Egyptians. Then he sent a terrible disease which killed their cattle.

Unrelenting, Pharaoh cried, 'I will not set the Israelites free!'

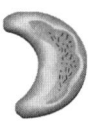

This time God afflicted the Egyptians with loathsome skin boils. He rained enormous hailstones down from heaven, destroying all the trees, and sent clouds of locusts which ate up all their crops.

Finally, God covered the land of Egypt in a dreadful darkness.

'Now will you let my people go?' Moses begged Pharaoh.

'No!' Pharaoh replied stubbornly. 'I will never let them go!'

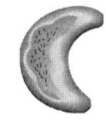

Exodus 6–10

Frogs in Rivers of Blood

Ingredients (serves 4)

1 x 135g packet **strawberry jelly (makes 550ml/1 pint)**

4 **kiwi fruits (make sure they're quite firm)**

black-and-white liquorice allsort rolls

multi-coloured dolly mixtures

chocolate sugar strands for sprinkling

1. Make up the jelly according to the packet instructions.
2. Peel the kiwis.
3. Cut each one in half lengthways and lay them cut side down on a chopping board.
4. Using a sharp knife, cut out the frogs' 'mouths' (the cutting instructions sound tricky but they are actually very simple). Make sure you cut the mouth on the **widest** side of the kiwi. First make a vertical (downwards) cut about 1/3 of the way back, and keeping in the middle of the kiwi (the cut should be about 2–4cm/1–1 1/2 in long). Do not cut right across and only take the knife halfway down.
5. Next, make a horizontal (sideways) cut at right angles to the first cut, so that a small wedge can be sliced out (see picture).
6. Cut a black-and-white liquorice allsort roll in half or use two dolly mixture sweets for the eyes. Place them on top of the 'frog' a little way back from the mouth and as far apart as possible. Repeat for all the frogs. Sprinkle a few chocolate sugar strands over the frogs' heads.
7. Chop up the jelly with a fork and spread over a large, flat serving dish. Place the frogs on top and serve.

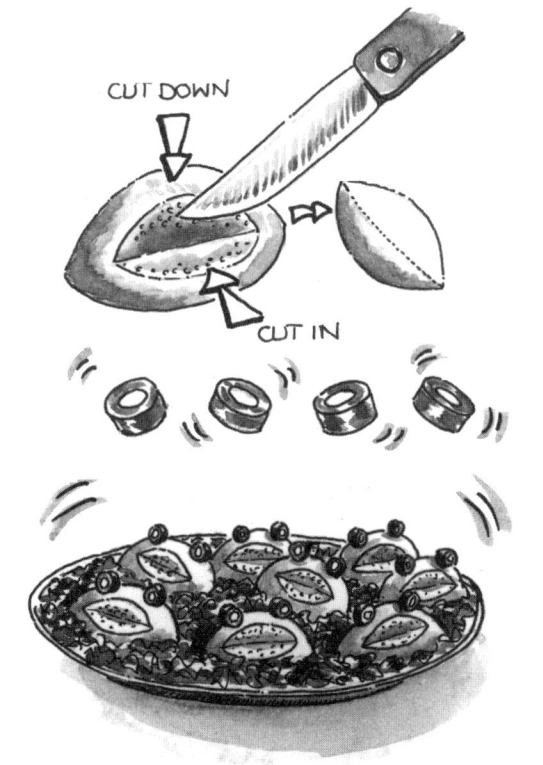

8. THE LAST PLAGUE

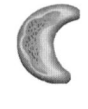

God told Moses, 'I will send one last terrible plague to Pharaoh. After that he will let you go. Tonight, I will kill every first-born man, woman and child in Egypt. Even their first-born cattle will die – but not one Israelite shall be harmed.'

Moses told his people what they must do to escape the plague. 'Each household must kill a lamb and daub its blood against the doorpost of the house. You shall then roast the lamb and eat it with unleavened bread and bitter herbs.'

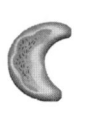

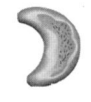

The people did this, staying tightly shut inside their homes. At midnight the Lord went through the land, killing the Egyptians. But he 'passed over' the houses belonging to the Israelites, and all were spared.

Suddenly the sound of loud wailing and screaming filled the air. The Egyptians were distraught. Death was everywhere. In his grief, Pharaoh sent for Moses. 'Take your people and go!' he cried. 'Get out of my country!'

Hastily the Israelites left. On that day God's promise to save them was fulfilled.

Exodus 11–12

THE JEWISH PASSOVER

God told the children of Israel that they must remember the exodus from Egypt by celebrating it as a feast day for ever. The feast day is called Pesach (which means 'passed over').

Jewish people still celebrate the feast to this day. Families prepare a special meal – called a Seder – for the Passover ceremony. It is one of the nicest occasions in Jewish family life, as many members get together for this meal.

The foods they eat remind the Jewish people of their captivity and slavery in Egypt, and how God set them free. Only unleavened bread (bread made with dough without yeast, so it doesn't rise) is eaten during Pesach. This reminds the Jews that as they left Egypt in a hurry, there was not time for their bread to rise.

THE SEDER PLATE
1. Matzos (unleavened bread). The matzo resembles a large cracker.
2. The roasted shank bone of a lamb. This is in memory of the Paschal lamb that was offered as a sacrifice at the time of the Jewish Temple. It is not eaten.
3. A hard-boiled egg. A reminder of the festival offering the Israelites offered in the temple. The egg's round shape symbolizes the wheel of destiny that the temple should be rebuilt.
4. Bitter herbs – usually horseradish. A symbol of the bitterness of slavery.
5. A green vegetable (parsley or celery). This is dipped in the salt water.
6. Charoset (see recipe, page 28). A symbol of the mortar the Israelites used to build bricks in Egypt.
7. A second 'set' of bitter herbs used in a sandwich of matzos, as opposed to the other bitter herbs that are eaten alone. Lettuce is often used.

ALSO ON THE SEDER TABLE:
8. A dish of salt water. This represents the tears shed by the Israelites while they were slaves.
9. Everyone drinks four cups of wine (they are drunk at different stages in the meal). A spare cup called 'Elijah's Goblet' is also placed on the table. According to Jewish tradition, Elijah the prophet 'visits' each Jewish home to bring the message of redemption on the night of freedom.

Charoset

Ingredients (a special recipe for Passover)

- 500g/1lb **apples**
- 50g/2oz **almonds**
- 50g/2oz **raisins**
- **cinnamon powder** (to taste)

1. Peel and core the apples. Chop finely and put in a bowl.
2. Chop the almonds and raisins, and mix them with the apple pieces.
3. Add a sprinkle of cinnamon to taste.
4. Roll the mixture into tiny balls.

Cinnamon Balls

Ingredients (this favourite Passover recipe makes about 24)

- 2 **large egg whites**
- 225g/8oz **ground almonds**
- 100g/4oz **caster sugar**
- 1 level tablespoon **ground cinnamon**
- **icing sugar for dusting**

You will need 2 non-stick baking sheets.

1. Pre-heat the oven to gas mark 3, 170°C (325°F).
2. Grease the baking sheets well.
3. Beat the egg whites in a bowl until they form stiff peaks.
4. Fold in the ground almonds, caster sugar and ground cinnamon.
5. With damp hands, form the mixture into small balls.
6. Place the balls on the baking sheets and bake for 25 minutes until just firm to the touch. Don't overbake or they will be ruined!
7. Allow to cool for 5 minutes, and then roll in the icing sugar.

Matzo Fritters

Ingredients (Based on a traditional Passover recipe. Serves 4. Try these – you'll really love them!)

- 4 **matzos**
- approx. 250ml/8floz **milk**
- 1 **egg**
- 2–3 tablespoons **oil, or**
- 25g/1oz **lard for frying**
- **cinnamon powder for sprinkling**
- **granulated sugar for sprinkling**
- 1 **lemon cut into slices**

Matzos can be bought in most large supermarkets. Look among the crispbreads or try the delicatessen or kosher sections.

1. Break the matzos into small pieces and place in a bowl. Pour over enough milk to cover them.
2. Leave the matzos to soak for 5 minutes or until they are soft. Meanwhile, beat the egg in a large bowl.
3. Drain the matzos and add to the egg.
4. Melt the lard or heat the oil in a frying-pan. Then, taking small dessertspoonfuls at a time, fry the matzo fritters for 2–3 minutes each side, until browned. Turn carefully using tongs. Don't worry if they fall apart – they'll still taste delicious!
5. Turn off the heat and place the fritters straight onto a plate.
6. Sprinkle generously with cinnamon and sugar and serve with slices of lemon. Eat piping hot.

9. FOOD IN THE DESERT

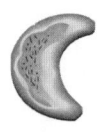

God led the Israelites through the Red Sea and into the desert. As they travelled onwards, their supplies of food soon ran out, and no more could be found.

'We should have stayed in Egypt,' the people complained to Moses. 'At least there was plenty to eat. Now we shall all starve.'

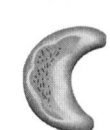

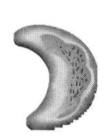

God heard their cries and told Moses, 'I will rain down bread from heaven for you all. The people must go out each morning and gather all they need for that day, and no more. But on the sixth day they may collect enough food for two days, so they will be able to rest on the Sabbath and keep it holy.'

The next morning, the Israelites found fine white flakes covering the ground, like frost.

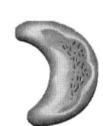

'What is it?' they asked.

'It is the food the Lord has given you,' Moses told them.

The people named their new food 'manna'. It tasted like wafers made with honey.

Exodus 16–17

'Manna' Ices

Ingredients

1 litre block	**vanilla ice-cream**
1 packet	**ice-cream wafers**
a little	**clear honey**

1. For each 'manna' ice, cut a thinnish slice of ice-cream from the block and lay it on top of a wafer.
2. Drizzle a little honey over the ice-cream and place a second wafer on top.
3. Drizzle some more honey over this wafer and place a second thinnish slice of ice-cream on top.
4. Sandwich it all together with a third wafer.
5. Serve at once.

10. A LAND FLOWING WITH MILK AND HONEY

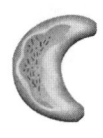

Moses and the Israelites wandered through the hot, dry, dusty desert, setting up camps as they went. They were headed for the land that God had promised them, Canaan.

'You shall inherit the land,' God told his people. 'I will give it to you as a country of your own. It is a good land – a land flowing with milk and honey.'

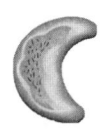

God then explained what he wanted from his people so that all would go well with them in their new home.

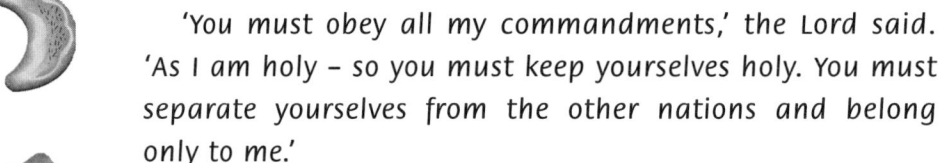

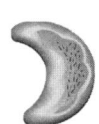

'You must obey all my commandments,' the Lord said. 'As I am holy – so you must keep yourselves holy. You must separate yourselves from the other nations and belong only to me.'

Leviticus 20

Milk and Honey Ice-cream

Ingredients (this deliciously rich and creamy ice-cream makes about 600ml/1 pint)

2	**egg yolks**
1	**egg white**
375ml/12fl oz	**milk**
175g/6oz	**clear runny honey**
250ml/8fl oz	**single cream**

You will need an ice-cream freezer container.

1. Put the egg yolks and egg white into a heatproof bowl. Whisk with a fork or hand-whisk until pale and creamy.
2. Heat the milk in a pan until hot. Add the honey, and stir well, but do not allow it to boil.
3. Pour the honey mixture into the egg mixture, and mix everything together.
4. Place the heatproof bowl over a saucepan of simmering water and cook gently, stirring slowly all the time, for about 30 minutes or until it thickens and begins to coat the back of a wooden spoon. Do not allow the mixture to boil or it will become lumpy.
5. When thickened, remove from heat. Stir in the cream and allow to cool.
6. Pour into the ice-cream freezer container and freeze for 4–6 hours until firm.

Milk and Honey Dreamy Desert Drink

Ingredients (serves 4)

750ml/1½ pints	**milk**
3 tablespoons	**runny honey**
a few drops	**rum essence (optional)**

1. Heat the milk in a large pan.
2. When hot, stir in the honey (and rum essence if you wish).
3. Serve immediately in mugs or tumblers.

Milk and Honey Fluff

Ingredients (serves 4)

half a 135g packet	**lemon jelly**
170g/6oz can	**evaporated milk, chilled**
1½ tablespoons	**clear honey**

You will need to chill the evaporated milk in the fridge for at least 4–5 hours before starting this recipe – this enables it to whip up properly.

1. Make up the jelly according to the packet instructions, remembering to halve any ingredients so that you make a 300ml/½ pint jelly. Put in the fridge and leave until half set. It should be wobbly but not solid.
2. Pour the evaporated milk into a bowl. Whisk with an electric whisk on the highest setting until it increases to twice the amount and looks like thick cream.
3. Add the honey and whisk again for a minute.
4. Add the jelly to the bowl, whisking on the lowest setting until it has blended in.
5. Pour into a large dish and leave in the fridge to set.
6. Serve piled into tall glasses.

11. THE FRUITS OF THE PROMISED LAND

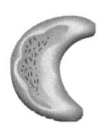

God told Moses, 'Send some of your men ahead to Canaan to spy out the land.'

So Moses chose leaders from each of the twelve tribes. 'Go and find out what our new country is like,' he told them. 'Discover if the land is rich or poor, and whether there are plenty of trees for wood.'

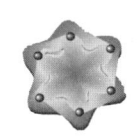

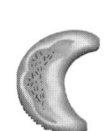

Moses also instructed the spies to bring back the fruits of the land.

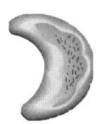

On their explorations, the men came to the Valley of Eshcol. At that time it was the season of the first fruit harvest. The grapes hung heavy on the vines and the men cut down a single cluster of them. It was so heavy that two men were needed to carry it back between them, hung over a pole! There were also plentiful supplies of pomegranates and figs and the men picked these too.

'Canaan is a rich country – flowing with milk and honey,' the spies reported to Moses on their return. 'Look, here are the fruits of our Promised Land!'

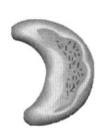

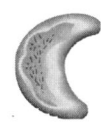

Numbers 13

Figgy Flapjacks

Ingredients (makes about 15)

50g/2oz	**dried, ready-to-eat-figs**
50g/2oz	**dried, ready-to-eat apricots**
350g/12oz	**porridge oats (not the 'quick' variety)**
pinch	**salt**
1 level teaspoon	**ground cinnamon**
150g/5oz	**demerara sugar**
175g/6oz	**butter or margarine**
1 tablespoon	**golden syrup**

You will need a 20 x 25cm (8 x 10in) shallow baking tin.

1. Pre-heat the oven to gas mark 5, 190°C (375°F).
2. Grease the shallow baking tin.
3. Roughly chop the dried apricots and dried figs, and set aside.
4. Put the porridge oats, salt, cinnamon and sugar into a large mixing bowl. Stir together.
5. Gently warm the butter (or margarine) and golden syrup in a saucepan. Stir together until the butter has melted. Add the chopped apricots and figs.
6. Pour the butter and fruit mixture in with the porridge oats mixture. Mix thoroughly.
7. Place the mixture into the prepared baking tin. Press down firmly with the back of a spoon.
8. Bake in the middle of the oven for about 25 minutes.
9. Remove from the oven and allow to cool a little before cutting into squares with a sharp knife.
10. Remove from the tin when cold.

Bible Fruits Compote

Ingredients (serves 4–6)

225g/½lb	**mixed red and white grapes**
1	**pomegranate**
1	**small honeydew or galia melon**
411g/14oz tin	**figs in syrup**
	water
	sugar to taste

1. First, prepare the fruit. Cut the grapes in half and remove any pips. Quarter the pomegranate and take out the red seeds. Slice the melon into quarters and remove the seeds. Use a melon baller to scoop out the flesh or, alternatively, cut into bite-sized chunks.
2. Put all the prepared fruit into a large saucepan.
3. Add the figs to the saucepan, draining the syrup from the tin into a measuring jug.
4. Add enough water to the measuring jug so that you have 300ml/½ pint. Add sugar to taste.
5. Add the syrup water to the saucepan of fruit. Heat gently until just warm and any sugar is dissolved. Remove from heat; the fruit should not be cooked.
6. The compote can be eaten immediately, or left to cool and served later. It's delicious with thick cream!

12. AARON'S STAFF

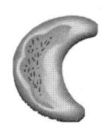

Aaron, the brother of Moses, was told by God, 'I have chosen you and your sons to serve me as my holy priests.'

However, this angered some of the other Israelites. 'Isn't every man holy before God?' they cried to Moses. 'Who says Aaron is so special?'

When God heard their complaints he commanded Moses, 'Tell the leaders from each of the twelve tribes of Israel to bring you their staffs. Write the name of each man on his own staff and write Aaron's name on his staff too. I will make the staff of the man I choose to serve me sprout leaves. That will put an end to the people's grumbling.'

Moses did as the Lord asked. The following day Aaron's staff had sprouted not only leaves and blossom, but ripe almonds too!

'See this!' Moses showed the Israelites. 'Only Aaron's staff has sprouted. Now you know that the Lord has chosen him – and him alone.'

Numbers 17

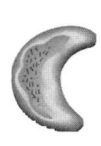

Aaron's Almond Shortbread

Ingredients	(makes 16–20 pieces)
100g/4oz	**ground rice**
200g/7oz	**plain flour**
25g/1oz	**cornflour**
100g/4oz	**caster sugar**
	(extra for sprinkling)
225g/8oz	**butter or margarine**
pinch	**salt**
½ teaspoon	**almond essence**

You will need 2 18cm/7in round cake tins.

1. Pre-heat the oven to gas mark 3, 170°C (325°F).
2. Grease the two cake tins.
3. Measure all the ingredients together into a large bowl.
4. Using your fingers or a pastry blender, work the mixture together until it binds.
5. Divide equally between the 2 tins, pressing the mixture down into the tins with your knuckles.
6. Lightly prick all over with a fork.
7. Bake in the middle of the oven for 50 minutes to 1 hour.
8. Sprinkle with caster sugar and cut into pieces while still warm. Remove from the tins when cold.

Almond and Raisin Fudge

Ingredients (makes about ¾ lb)
- 25g/1oz **blanched almonds**
- 25g/1oz **seedless raisins**
- 25g/1oz **butter**
- 2 tablespoons **water**
- 1 tablespoon **golden syrup**
- 225g/8oz **granulated sugar**
- 4 tablespoons **evaporated milk**
- ½ teaspoon **vanilla essence**

You will need a small, square tin.

1. If you can't find blanched almonds, then remove their skins by putting the nuts in a basin of boiling water, leaving them for a few minutes and then straining and peeling off the skins.
2. Chop the almonds into small pieces, roughly chop up the raisins and set both aside.
3. Grease the small, square tin.
4. Put all the other ingredients **except** for the vanilla essence, almonds and raisins into a large, heavy-based saucepan.
5. Using a wooden spoon, stir the ingredients gently over a low heat until all the sugar dissolves.
6. Bring to the boil. Allow to boil very gently for about 10 minutes, stirring all the time to prevent burning. The mixture is ready when it begins to thicken slightly and when it forms a soft ball when a few drops are placed in a saucer of cold water.
7. Remove the pan from the heat. Add the vanilla essence, almonds and raisins.
8. Beat the mixture with the wooden spoon until it thickens further. Don't overdo it or the fudge will be dry and crumbly!
9. Quickly pour into the tin. Cut into squares while still warm.

13. BARAK'S VICTORIOUS BATTLE

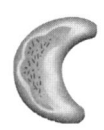

After wandering in the desert for 40 years, the Israelites finally reached Canaan. As life grew easier, the people forgot God and worshipped idols instead.

God was saddened and let them be taken over by their enemies, the Canaanites, led by a cruel commander called Sisera.

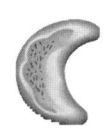

At that time, Israel was ruled by the prophetess Deborah. God told her to summon a man called Barak.

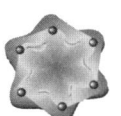

'The Lord wants you to fight the Canaanites,' Deborah told Barak. 'Gather 10,000 soldiers and march to the River Kishon. Sisera's army will meet you there.'

Barak was terrified. 'Sisera has 900 chariots, but we have none!' he cried. 'We'll lose the battle!'

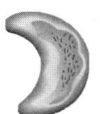

Barak only agreed to go if Deborah came too. As Sisera's army charged towards Barak's men, God sent a violent downpour. The ground became a sticky, muddy swamp.

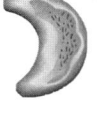

'Our chariots can't move,' cried Sisera's soldiers. 'We're stuck in the mud!'

As the Canaanites advanced on foot, the river burst its banks. Sisera's army was swept away in the flood and utterly destroyed. Not one man was left alive.

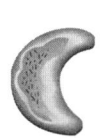

Judges 4

Sisera's 'Stuck in the Mud' Pudding

Ingredients (this scrummy, sticky chocolate fudge pudding serves 4)

140g/5oz	**self-raising flour**
4 tablespoons	**cocoa powder**
50g/2oz	**caster sugar**
large pinch	**salt**
2 tablespoons	**melted butter or margarine**
140ml/5 fl oz	**milk**
½ teaspoon	**vanilla essence**
140g/5oz	**demerara sugar**
50g/2oz	**chopped walnuts (optional)**
280ml/10 fl oz	**boiling water**

1. Pre-heat the oven to gas mark 4, 180°C (350°F).
2. Grease a large baking dish.
3. Sift the flour and 2 tablespoons of the cocoa powder into a bowl. Add the chopped walnuts if you are using them.
4. Stir in the caster sugar and salt.
5. Add the butter (or margarine) that has been melted in a separate saucepan, milk and vanilla essence. Mix well and pour into the baking dish.
6. In another bowl, mix together the demerara sugar and remaining 2 tablespoons of cocoa powder. Sprinkle over the top of the pudding.
7. Pour over the boiling water and bake in the oven for about 45 minutes. This pud makes its own delicious 'mud' sauce, so get stuck in!

Sisera's Chariot-Wheel Quiche

Ingredients (serves 4)

For the pastry

225g/8oz	**plain flour**
pinch	**salt**
100g/4oz	**soft margarine**
approx. 2–4 tablespoons	**water**

For the filling

345g/12 fl oz tin	**whole asparagus spears**
1	**small onion**
3	**eggs**
120ml/4floz	**milk**
	salt and pepper
50g/2oz	**cheddar cheese, grated**
1	**olive (green or black)**

You will need a 20cm/8in flan dish.

1. Pre-heat the oven to gas mark 7, 220°C (425°F).
2. First, make the pastry. Sieve the flour and salt into a mixing bowl.
3. Cut the margarine into small pieces and add to the flour. Rub the margarine into the flour using your fingers until the mixture looks like fine breadcrumbs.
4. Make a well in the centre. Add the water a little at a time, blending in with a knife and then your hands until it forms a firm, dryish dough.
5. Knead the pastry lightly, then, on a surface sprinkled with flour, roll out to about 5mm/¼in thick. Line the greased flan dish with the pastry, pressing down firmly.
6. Drain the asparagus well. Choose 8 nice whole spears and put them to one side for later. Chop the rest into small pieces and lay evenly at the bottom of the flan dish.
7. Chop the onion finely. Sprinkle over the asparagus pieces. Then sprinkle the cheese on top.
8. Break the eggs into a bowl. Add the salt and pepper and beat well. Stir in the milk and pour the whole mixture over the asparagus, onion and cheese.
9. Place the flan dish on a baking tray and

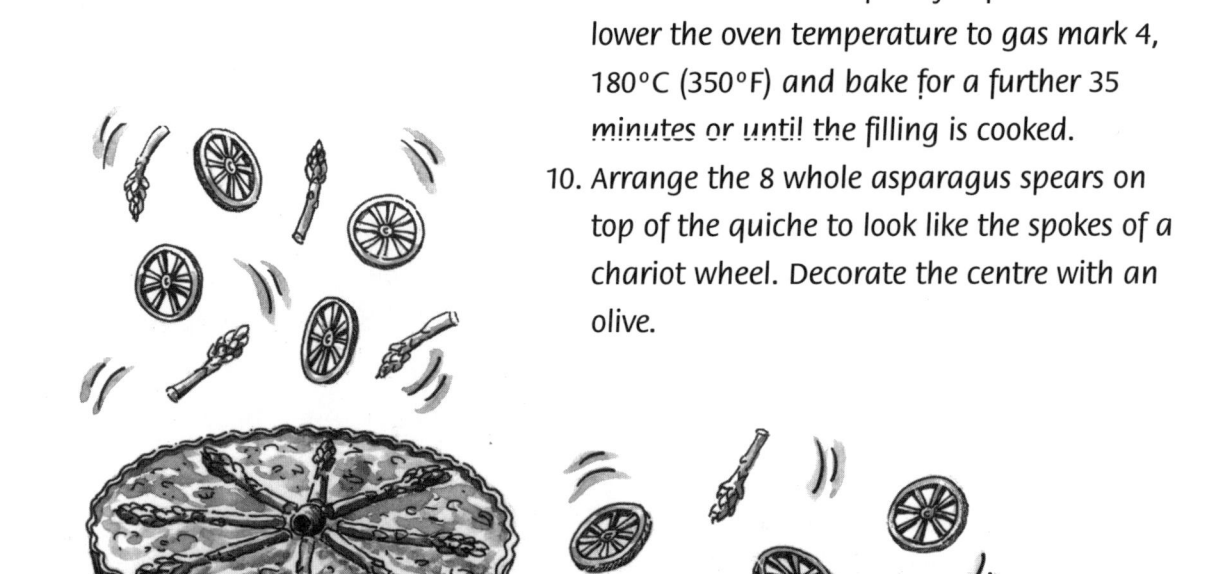

cook in the middle of the oven for about 25 minutes or until the pastry is firm. Then lower the oven temperature to gas mark 4, 180°C (350°F) and bake for a further 35 minutes or until the filling is cooked.

10. Arrange the 8 whole asparagus spears on top of the quiche to look like the spokes of a chariot wheel. Decorate the centre with an olive.

Mudslide Shakes

Ingredients (makes 4 glasses)

2	**bananas**
750ml/ 1½ pints	**milk**
4 level tablespoons	**chocolate-flavoured syrup topping**

1. Slice the bananas and place in a liquidizer or blender. Whisk until smooth.
2. Add the milk and chocolate syrup topping. Whisk again until it has blended.
3. Pour into glasses and serve with a straw.

-44-

14. THE STORY OF RUTH

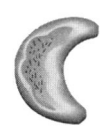

Naomi, an Israelite woman, lived in Moab. Her two sons married two Moabite women called Orpah and Ruth.

There was a terrible famine in the land and Naomi's husband – and her sons – died.

'I shall return alone to my home in Bethlehem,' Naomi told her daughters-in-law sorrowfully. 'You stay here where you belong.'

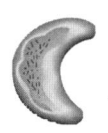

Orpah agreed, but Ruth loved Naomi and begged to go with her. 'Where you go, I will go; your people shall be my people, and your God will be my God,' she said.

The two women arrived in Bethlehem at harvest time. It so happened that one of Naomi's relatives, a rich man called Boaz, owned one of the barley fields. So Ruth went into his fields to gather the grain left behind by the workers, and Boaz spotted her.

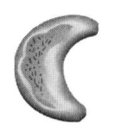

'Who is she?' he asked his servants. 'Naomi's daughter-in-law,' they replied.

Hearing how loyal Ruth had been to Naomi, Boaz showed her extra kindness by letting her take home as many bundles of grain as she liked.

Eventually Ruth and Boaz married. One of their sons was the grandfather of David – Israel's greatest king.

Ruth

Ruth's Straw Bundles

Ingredients (makes about 6 bundles)

- 100g/4oz **plain flour**
- 50g/2oz **butter**
- 75g/3oz **grated strong cheddar cheese**
- pinch **salt, pepper, cayenne pepper**
- 1 **egg yolk**

You will need a large baking tray, and 2 biscuit cutters (different sizes).

1. Pre-heat the oven to gas mark 6, 200°C (400°F).
2. Grease and flour a large baking tray.
3. Sift the flour into a bowl. Rub in the butter until the mixture resembles fine breadcrumbs.
4. Stir in the cheese and the salt, pepper and cayenne pepper. Add the egg yolk and bind the mixture together with your fingers to make a firm dough. If necessary add a tiny amount of water.
5. Roll out the dough on a board sprinkled with flour to a thickness of about 5mm/¼in. Cut into short straws around 8cm/3in long and 5mm/¼in wide.
6. Re-roll any dough you haven't used, and cut out rings using the 2 different sized biscuit cutters. (You will need 1 ring for each 3–4 straws.)
7. Place on the baking tray and cook for 10–15 minutes until lightly browned.
8. Remove the straws carefully from the tray and put 3–4 straws through each ring to serve.

15. KING SOLOMON

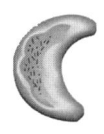

When King David died, his son Solomon became ruler of Israel. One night, God appeared to King Solomon in a dream.

'What do you want from me?' God asked.

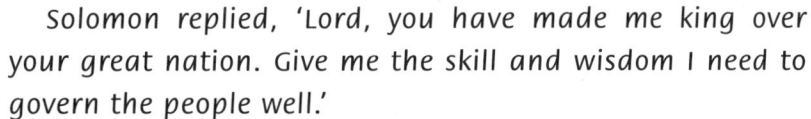

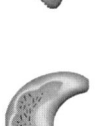

Solomon replied, 'Lord, you have made me king over your great nation. Give me the skill and wisdom I need to govern the people well.'

God was very pleased with this reply. 'Because you have asked nothing for yourself – be it long life, riches, or victory over your enemies,' he said, 'I will grant you your wish, and also give you riches and honour beyond compare.'

God kept his word to Solomon. Never before had a king been so wise, or so rich and powerful.

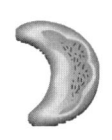

Solomon used his immense wealth to build a magnificent temple to God. No expense was spared. Cedar trees were shipped in from Lebanon. The costliest stones were used. Everything inside the temple was made of gold – even the walls were covered in pure gold.

The temple took seven years to build, and with great joy and celebration all the people came to worship God.

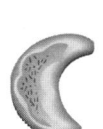

1 Kings 2–9

Solomon's Golden Shields

Ingredients (Tasty and easy to make pizza baps. Makes 12)

6	**white or wholemeal baps**
1 x 400g tin	**chopped tomatoes**
	oregano
1 x 50g tin	**anchovy fillets (in olive oil)**
200g/7oz	**grated medium to strong cheddar cheese**
12	**black olives**

You will need 2 large baking trays.

1. Pre-heat the oven to gas mark 5, 190°C (375°F).
2. Cover the baking trays with greaseproof paper.
3. Slice the baps in half and lay on the baking trays, cut surfaces up.
4. Spoon the chopped tomatoes (and juice) evenly over the tops of the baps. Spread right to the edges.
5. Sprinkle each bap with oregano.
6. Divide the anchovy fillets between the baps, placing them on top.
7. Sprinkle the cheese over each bap.
8. Garnish each bap with a black olive.
9. Bake in the middle of the oven for around 20–25 minutes or until the baps are golden brown.
10. Serve hot with a green salad or coleslaw, and crisps.

Solomon's Bowls of Gold

Ingredients (serves 4)

For the cups

4	**small oranges**
32	**whole raspberries or blackberries**
4 teaspoons	**sugar**

For the meringue

4	**egg whites**
2 tablespoons	**caster sugar**
	extra sugar for sprinkling

1. Pre-heat the oven to gas mark 3, 170°C (325°F).
2. Wash the oranges and cut in half widthways.
3. Using a grapefruit knife, slice all the way round the orange halves cutting just inside the fruit so as to separate the peel from the fruit completely. Try not to pierce the skins. The orange fruit can then easily be separated from the pith and pips with the knife.
4. Once all the pith and pips have been removed, pile the orange segments back into the empty cups. Place the cups in a shallow dish, close together so they don't topple over.
5. Put four raspberries or blackberries in each cup. Sprinkle ½ teaspoon of sugar over each one.
6. Now make the meringues. Whisk the egg whites until they are very stiff.
7. Fold in the 2 tablespoons of sugar, and whisk again.
8. Pile the meringue on top of the orange cups. Sprinkle with a little more sugar.
9. Cook in the middle of the oven for 15–20 minutes until the meringues are golden. Serve hot.

King's Royal Crowns

Ingredients (makes about 23 biscuits)

For the biscuits

175g/6oz	**self-raising flour**
100g/4oz	**granulated sugar**
100g/4oz	**butter or margarine**
1	**large egg, beaten**
½ teaspoon	**vanilla essence**

For the decoration

175g/6oz	**icing sugar**
6–10 teaspoons	**hot water**
	edible silver balls
	tiny sweets
	red and yellow food colouring

You will need a small piece of card to make a 'crown' template, 2 large baking sheets, and a piping bag and nozzle.

1. Pre-heat the oven to gas mark 6, 200°C (400°F).
2. Grease and flour the 2 baking sheets.
3. Place the flour, sugar and butter (or margarine) in a bowl. Rub together with your fingers until the mixture looks like breadcrumbs.
4. Add the beaten egg and vanilla essence. Knead together to form a soft dough.
5. On a surface sprinkled with flour, roll out the dough to a thickness of 5mm/¼in. Using your template cut out crown shapes with a sharp knife.
6. Place the crowns on the baking sheets and cook for 10–15 minutes, or until golden. Leave to cool on a wire rack.
7. Put the icing sugar into a bowl. Add the water one teaspoonful at a time until the icing becomes thick enough to pipe.
8. Divide the icing into 3 small bowls. Leave one white and colour the other 2 with a few drops of red and yellow food colouring.
9. Put the icing, one colour at a time, into a piping bag fitted with a plain writing nozzle. Pipe zig-zags, decorations or outlines on the crowns.
10. Decorate with silver balls or sweets and leave to set.

16. THE QUEEN OF SHEBA

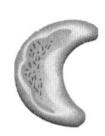

News of Solomon's greatness and wisdom spread far and wide. Soon the Queen of Sheba heard of his fame.

'I shall visit Solomon and see for myself if these rumours about him are true,' she decided.

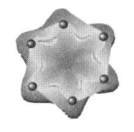

The queen travelled to Jerusalem, bringing with her hundreds of camels bearing spices, precious stones and much gold.

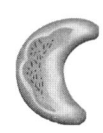

Solomon welcomed her warmly and the queen asked him many difficult questions, testing his wisdom. Solomon answered everything – nothing was too difficult for him.

Solomon then led the Queen of Sheba around his beautiful golden palaces, showing her his banqueting halls and magnificently dressed officials. She was breathless with admiration!

'What I heard of you is true,' she said. 'I would not believe it until I had seen it, but your wealth and wisdom exceed all the stories. Praise be to the Lord for giving Israel such a king.'

The queen gave Solomon gifts of gold, jewels and a great quantity of spices – such as had never been seen before. In return he gave her all she desired, and happily she departed to her own land.

1 Kings 10

The Queen of Sheba's "3 Spices" Honey Cake

Ingredients (Delicious sliced and buttered for tea)

225g/8oz	**self-raising flour**
100g/4oz	**granulated sugar**
1 level teaspoon	**ground mixed spice**
1 level teaspoon	**ground cinnamon**
1 level teaspoon	**ground nutmeg**
100g/¼lb	**runny honey**
150ml/¼ pint	**boiling water**

You will need a 226 x 105 x 57mm/1lb loaf tin.

1. Pre-heat the oven to gas mark 5, 190°C (375°F).
2. Grease the loaf tin well.
3. Sift the flour, sugar and mixed spice, cinnamon and nutmeg into a large bowl.
4. Melt the honey and water together in a saucepan. Bring to the boil.
5. Add the honey mixture to the dry ingredients and blend well using a wooden spoon.
6. Pour the mixture into the loaf tin and bake in the middle of the oven for about 1 hour, or until a skewer comes out clean from the centre. The cake should be well risen with a crusty top.
7. Remove from the tin while still warm and leave to cool on a wire rack. This cake improves after a day's keeping – if you can wait that long!

Cinnamon Toast

Ingredients

sliced fresh bread
butter for spreading
ground cinnamon powder
granulated sugar

1. Toast and butter the bread and cut off the crusts.
2. Sprinkle each slice generously with cinnamon.
3. Top with a sprinkling of sugar (about ½–1 teaspoon per slice), and spread with a knife.
4. Cut into small triangles and serve while hot.

Ginger Spiced Apples

Ingredients (serves 4)

4	**medium-sized cooking apples**
50g/2oz	**soft light brown sugar**
250ml/8fl oz	**water**
3–4 tablespoons	**ginger preserve or ginger marmalade**

1. Pre-heat the oven to gas mark 6, 200°C (400°F).
2. Core the apples and, using a sharp knife, score the skins all the way round the centre to prevent the apples from 'bursting' during cooking.
3. Stir the sugar and water together into an oven-proof dish. Sit the apples on top and fill the centres with the ginger preserve.
4. Bake in the middle of the oven for about 1 hour. Serve with cream.

17. ELIJAH AND THE BARREL OF CORN

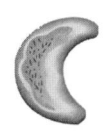

Time passed, and once again the Israelites turned away from God.

The Lord told his prophet Elijah, 'Tell the people that because of their wickedness there will be a terrible drought and famine in the land.'

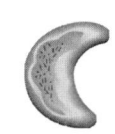

Then he instructed Elijah, 'Hide by the Cherith brook – I will feed you there.'

Elijah obeyed. He drank water from the brook and ravens brought him bread and meat to eat. But in time the brook dried up. 'Go to Sidon,' the Lord told him. 'There you will find help.'

Elijah reached the city tired and hungry. A poor woman was nearby gathering sticks, and Elijah begged her for food.

'I've nothing left,' she answered sadly. 'Just a little corn in a barrel and a small jar of oil. It will be the last meal my son and I eat.'

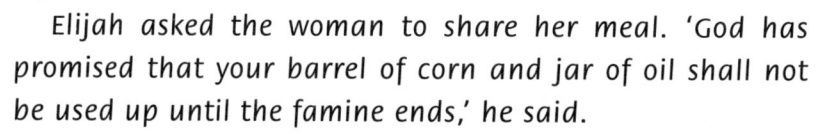

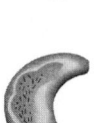

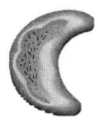

Elijah asked the woman to share her meal. 'God has promised that your barrel of corn and jar of oil shall not be used up until the famine ends,' he said.

God was true to his word – and there was always enough for the woman and her son to eat!

1 Kings 17

Elijah's Barrels of Corn

Ingredients (serves 4)

4	**medium-large green peppers**
1	**large carrot**
1	**large onion**
25g/1oz	**margarine for frying**
450g/1lb	**lamb mince**
	salt and pepper
	garlic powder (optional)
1 tablespoon	**tomato purée**
600ml/1 pint	**water reserved from pepper water**
1	**beef stock cube**
198g/17oz tin	**sweetcorn**

1. Pre-heat the oven to gas mark 4, 180°C (350°F).
2. Cut the tops off the peppers and carefully remove the cores and seeds.
3. Cook the peppers in a saucepan of boiling water for 5 minutes.
4. Remove from the pan and place in a casserole dish. Keep the pepper water for later.
5. Dice the carrot and onion. Using the margarine, fry together gently in a pan for a few minutes until the onions are golden.
6. Add the mince, salt, pepper (and garlic powder, if you wish) to the pan. Turn the meat well to ensure it is browned all over.
7. Turn down the heat. Add the tomato purée and the pepper water and crumble the stock cube over everything. Let it simmer for about 5 minutes.
8. Then stuff the peppers ¾ full with the meat and spoon the gravy and remaining meat around the bottom of the casserole dish.
9. Cover with a lid and bake in the oven for 40–45 minutes.
10. Five minutes before serving, heat up the sweetcorn separately in a dish in the oven.
11. Spoon the sweetcorn over the tops of the peppers so they look like barrels of corn, and serve. This is nice with rice!

18. THE STORY OF ESTHER

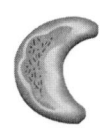

When Esther became queen to King Xerxes of Persia, she kept her Jewish faith a secret. But an official, named Haman, hated the Jews and came up with a plan to kill them.

'These people never obey your laws,' Haman lied to King Xerxes. 'They must be wiped out. Order them to be destroyed and I will pay 10,000 talents into the King's treasuries.'

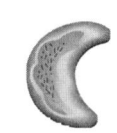

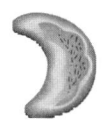

King Xerxes believed Haman and lots were drawn to decide on which day the Jews would perish.

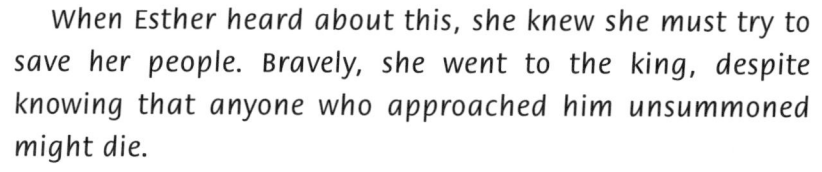

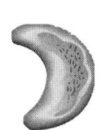

When Esther heard about this, she knew she must try to save her people. Bravely, she went to the king, despite knowing that anyone who approached him unsummoned might die.

The King listened to Esther's explanation of Haman's deception and was furious. 'Haman shall hang!' he decreed. 'By law the Jewish people may fight back and protect themselves on the allotted day of their destruction.'

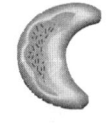

The Jews were overjoyed. They celebrated with a feast called Purim (meaning 'lots').

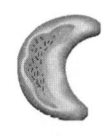

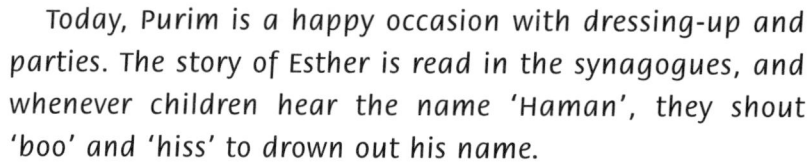

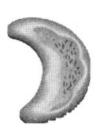

Today, Purim is a happy occasion with dressing-up and parties. The story of Esther is read in the synagogues, and whenever children hear the name 'Haman', they shout 'boo' and 'hiss' to drown out his name.

Esther

Hamantaschen ('Haman's Purses')

Ingredients (3-cornered pastries traditionally eaten at Purim. Makes 18.)

For the pastry

225g/8oz	**self-raising flour**
pinch	**salt**
75g/3oz	**granulated sugar**
75g/3oz	**soft margarine**
1	**egg**
approx. 1–2 tablespoons	**apple juice**

For the filling

50g/2oz	**poppy seeds**
40g/1½oz	**chopped walnuts**
40g/1½oz	**chopped raisins**
1 tablespoon	**golden syrup**
grated rind of ½	**lemon**
1 teaspoon	**lemon juice**
15g/½oz	**butter**
25g/1oz	**sugar**
2 tablespoons	**water**
	milk for brushing
	sugar for sprinkling

You will need 2 large, non-stick baking sheets, and a 7cm/3in pastry cutter.

1. First make the pastry. Sieve the flour, salt and sugar into a mixing bowl.
2. Rub in the margarine with your fingertips until the mixture looks like fine breadcrumbs.
3. Mix in the beaten egg and add enough apple juice to form the mixture into a soft dough when lightly kneaded.
4. Chill in the fridge for half an hour.
5. Meanwhile, make the filling. Put all the filling ingredients into a saucepan. Bring to the boil and cook over a gentle heat for 5–8 minutes until the mixture thickens. Turn off the heat and allow to cool completely.
6. Pre-heat the oven to gas mark 4, 180°C (350°F). Grease two large non-stick baking sheets.
7. On a surface sprinkled with flour, roll out the pastry to a thickness of ½cm/¼in. Using the cutter, press out circles.
8. Put a small teaspoonful of the filling in the centre of each pastry circle.
9. Fold the edges of the circle together and pinch firmly to form a triangle. Place on the baking sheets.
10. Brush each pastry lightly with milk and sprinkle with sugar.
11. Bake for 20–25 minutes, or until golden.
12. Wearing gloves, remove from the oven and leave to cool on a wire rack.

19. DANIEL IN THE LIONS' DEN

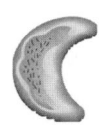

Daniel was highly favoured by King Darius the Mede, who put him in charge of the whole kingdom.

In their jealousy, the king's other officials plotted against him. These officials could find no fault in Daniel and so they planned to trick him. Knowing that Daniel prayed regularly to God, they visited King Darius with a plan.

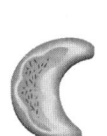

'O King,' they said. 'We advise you to make a new law. For the next 30 days, whoever prays to anyone but you must be thrown into the lions' den.'

King Darius signed the order. Daniel heard about it, but continued praying openly to God. Gleefully his enemies reported him.

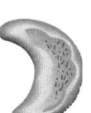

The king was greatly distressed and wanted to rescue Daniel. But the law stood fast and Daniel was thrown to the lions.

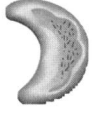

At daybreak, after a sleepless night praying, the king hurried to the lions' den. 'Has your God delivered you, Daniel?' he called down.

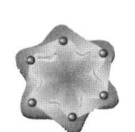

'God has shut the mouth of the lions,' Daniel replied. 'I am unhurt.'

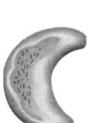

Joyfully, King Darius released Daniel, and no wounds were found on him because he had trusted in God.

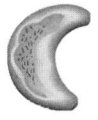

Daniel 6

Daniel's Roaring Lion Tarts

Ingredients (makes about 6 tarts)

175g/6oz	**plain flour**
pinch	**salt**
75g/3oz	**soft margarine**
approx. 3 dessert-spoonfuls	**water**
	jam (dark jam is best)
	milk (for brushing)
	sugar (for sprinkling)

You will need 1 jumbo straw, a jam tart baking tin, and 3 round crinkle cutters (1 small [55mm/2 in], 1 medium [65mm/2½in], and 1 large [75mm/3in]).

1. Pre-heat the oven to gas mark 7, 220°C (425°F).
2. Grease a jam tart baking tin.
3. First, make the pastry. Sift the flour and salt into a large bowl.
4. Rub in the margarine with your fingertips until the mixture looks like breadcrumbs.
5. Add the water, a little at a time, and mix with a blunt knife. When the dough begins to stick together, use your hands to form it into a ball.
6. Sprinkle flour onto a work surface. Roll out the pastry thinly on this surface.
7. Cut out 6 rounds using the **large** cutter. Press the circles gently on to the jam tart baking tray.
8. Fill the centres of each tart with one heaped teaspoon of jam. Brush the edges with some milk.
9. Using the **medium** sized cutter, press out 12 circles of pastry. Reserve 6 for the lions' manes. Lay the other 6 on top of each tart. Press around the edges with your fingers to seal the 2 circles, and brush with milk.
10. Now make the lions' manes. Using the **small** cutter, press out small circles **inside** the remaining 6 pastry rounds. Gently remove the inner circles and set aside for trimmings.

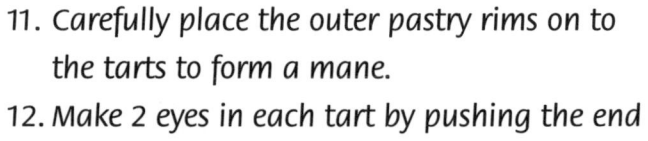

11. Carefully place the outer pastry rims on to the tarts to form a mane.
12. Make 2 eyes in each tart by pushing the end of a jumbo straw into the pastry. Make sure it goes in deep enough to show the jam underneath.
13. Use some of the remaining pastry trimmings to roll small 'noses' for the lions. Press gently into place.
14. Use a sharp knife to cut curved slits under each nose for the lions' mouths.
15. Re-roll the trimmings and cut out ears, a tongue and whiskers for each tart. To make the whiskers cut a thin oblong shape twice the length of each whisker. Cut in half. Make 2 slits in each side and fan the whiskers out.
16. Carefully lay the ears, tongue and whiskers in place. Brush with milk and sprinkle each tart with sugar. Bake for 15–20 minutes or until golden brown.

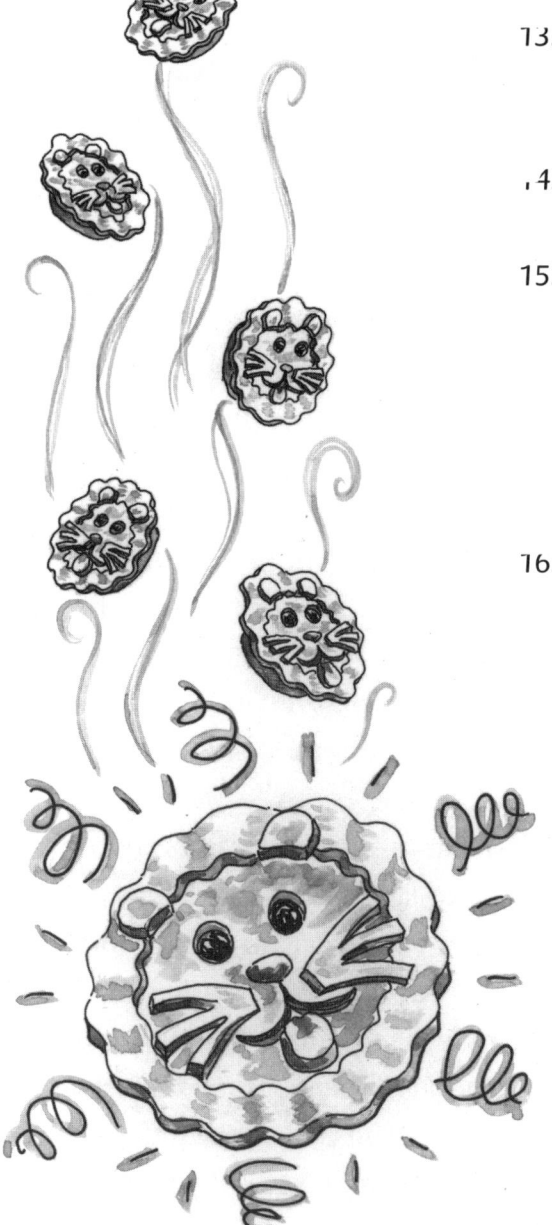

20. JONAH AND THE GREAT FISH

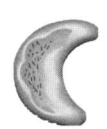

God told his prophet Jonah, 'Go to Nineveh. Warn its people to stop their wickedness or I will destroy the city.'

But Jonah was scared and refused. Instead, he boarded a ship sailing for Tarshish. God sent a great storm until the boat was in danger of breaking up. Terrified, the sailors drew lots to discover who was to blame for their trouble – and Jonah's name came up.

'Yes, the storm is my fault,' Jonah said. 'I've disobeyed God. Throw me overboard and the waves will die down.'

Jonah was thrown into the sea and the storm ceased. He sank and was swallowed by a huge fish. For three days he lay inside its stomach praying, 'Lord, save me.'

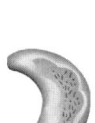

God commanded the fish to spit Jonah out on to dry land. Now Jonah obeyed and went to Nineveh. The people believed God's warning. They prayed for forgiveness and God spared them, making Jonah angry.

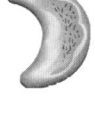

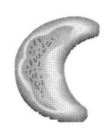

'Why should their sins be forgiven?' he grumbled.

Miserably he sat in the desert where God made a vine grow to shade him. But the next day the vine withered and died. Jonah became angry again, so God spoke to him.

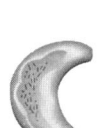

'You are concerned about a tree you didn't even nurture. Shouldn't I care for the many people of Nineveh?'

Jonah

Jonah's Fun Fish Cakes

Ingredients (makes about 12 little fish-shaped salmon patties)

1	**medium-size egg**
1 x 213g tin	**pink or red salmon**
pinch	**salt and pepper**
2–3 tablespoons	**medium or fine matzo meal**
	100% vegetable fat or vegetable oil for frying

1. Beat the egg in a large bowl.
2. Add the salmon and stir together. Season lightly with salt and pepper.
3. Add the matzo meal one spoon at a time. Mash with a fork until the mixture binds to a workable paste.
4. Take small amounts of the mixture and mould into small fish shapes.
5. Gently flatten the cakes with your hand, so that they are about 1cm/$^1/_2$in thick.
6. Heat the fat or oil in a large frying pan. Carefully put in the fish cakes using a spatula.
7. Let them cook on a gentle heat for about 5–6 minutes each side. Use tongs to turn them and handle gently.
8. Either serve at once or keep warm in the oven in a covered dish.

Jonah's Fish and Ships

Ingredients (serves 4)

50g/2oz **soft margarine (for basting)**

750g/1½lbs **potatoes (medium-large, even-shaped)**

salt and pepper

garlic granules

You will need a large, non-stick roasting tray.

1. Pre-heat the oven to gas mark 5, 190°C (375°F).
2. Put 25g/1oz of the margarine on to a large non-stick roasting tray. Put in the oven to melt.
3. Peel the potatoes. Cut lengthwise into roughly 6mm/¼in thick slices.
4. Cut out the ship shapes, and fish shapes. Round end-pieces can be made into starfish or octopus.
5. Take out the roasting tin from the oven. Carefully place the potato shapes on to the melted margarine. Season with salt, pepper and garlic granules. Dot on the remaining margarine.
6. Return the tray to the oven. After 5 minutes take out, and check that the shapes are well basted with the fat.
7. Bake for 1 hour, turning the shapes carefully half way through cooking time. They should be crisp and golden on the outside but soft in the middle.
8. Great served with Jonah's Fun Fish Cakes!

Deep Sea Jellies

Ingredients *(Makes a 600ml/1 pint jelly)*

3 tablespoons	**hot water**
11.7g sachet/ 1 tablespoon	**gelatine**
600ml/1 pint	**clear apple juice**
few drops	**blue food colouring**
100g/4oz	**assorted coloured jelly sweets**

1. Put the hot water in a bowl. Sprinkle over the gelatine powder and stir briskly until well mixed. Place the bowl over a pan of hot water until the gelatine dissolves.
2. Add the apple juice and a few drops of blue food colouring to the bowl.
3. Pour the jelly between 4 individual transparent cups or moulds.
4. With a sharp knife, slice the jelly sweets in half. Cut some jellies into thin strips to make seaweed. Roughly cut the other jellies into simple fish or shell shapes.
5. When the jellies in the moulds have half set, drop in the sweets.
6. Chill in the fridge until set.